First Facts® U.S. NATIONAL PARKS
FIELD GUIDES

YOSEMITE
NATIONAL PARK

by Megan Cooley Peterson

PEBBLE
a capstone imprint

First Facts Books are published by Pebble,
1710 Roe Crest Drive, North Mankato, Minnesota 56003
www.mycapstone.com

Library of Congress Cataloging-in-Publication Data is available
on the Library of Congress website.
ISBN 978-1-9771-0357-4 (library binding)
ISBN 978-1-9771-0527-1 (paperback)
ISBN 978-1-9771-0364-2 (ebook pdf)

Editorial Credits:
Anna Butzer, editor
Juliette Peters, designer
Tracy Cummins, media researcher
Kathy McColley, production specialist

Photo Credits:
Capstone: Eric Gohl, 7, 10 Bottom, 13, 15 Bottom, 17 Bottom;
iStockphoto: Bobbushphoto, 11 Top; Library of Congress: 8;
Shutterstock: Aspen Photo, Cover Bottom Left, Boris Edelmann,
2–3, 6–7, 11 Bottom, brm, 17 Top, canadastock, 5 Top, Carl
Player, Back Cover, Cover Top, Cat_arch_angel, Design Element,
Christine Krahl, Design Element, Christophe Testi, 3 Bottom,
Colin D. Young, 19 Right, 19 Left, davidhoffmann photography,
3 Middle, Gary C. Tognoni, 12–13, Glen C, 3 Top, Jason Finn, 10
Left, KanokpolTokumhnerd, Design Element, Kelly vanDellen, 18
Bottom, kyle post photography, 20, Laurens Hoddenbagh, Cover
Bottom Middle, Lorcel, Cover Bottom Right, Lynn Yeh, 14 Left,
Onnes, 1, Oscity, 9, Papatpong Phermsang-ngarm, 22–23, 24, Robert
Bohrer, 14 Right, robert cicchetti, 16–17, shaferaphoto, 21 Bottom,
Stephen Moehle, 5 Bottom, Tom Grundy, 18–19, vagabond54, 21
Top, viewgene, Design Element, Vlad Klok, Design Element, Yongyut
Kumsri, 15 Top

Printed and bound in the USA.
1335

Table of Contents

Welcome to Yosemite

Yosemite National Park is one of the most famous parks in North America. The park covers more than 1,100 square miles (2,850 square kilometers) in the Sierra Nevada Mountains. The U.S. government set the land aside as a national park in 1890.

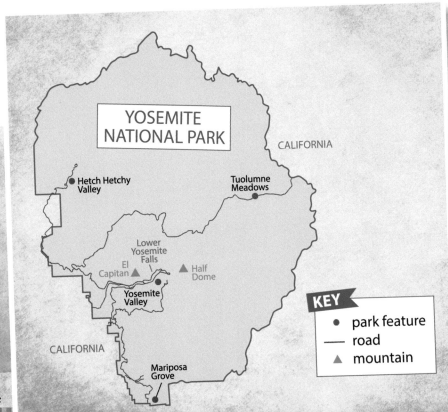

YOSEMITE NATIONAL PARK

CALIFORNIA

Hetch Hetchy Valley

Tuolumne Meadows

Lower Yosemite Falls

El Capitan ▲

▲ Half Dome

Yosemite Valley

CALIFORNIA

Mariposa Grove

KEY
- • park feature
- — road
- ▲ mountain

Yosemite Valley

Yosemite's land was created by **glaciers**. These large sheets of ice moved through the Yosemite **Valley** 1 million years ago. They shaped the land and left behind **landmarks**. Some of these landmarks include Yosemite Valley, Hetch Hetchy, Yosemite Falls, and Half Dome.

FACT: The rare Yosemite bog orchid grows only in the Yosemite Valley. Many black oak trees also grow here. Bears, deer, woodpeckers, and squirrels eat the acorns from black oak trees.

Cook's Meadow is in the middle of Yosemite Valley. Visitors can walk around the meadow on the Cook's Meadow Loop. It is only 1 mile (1.6 km) long.

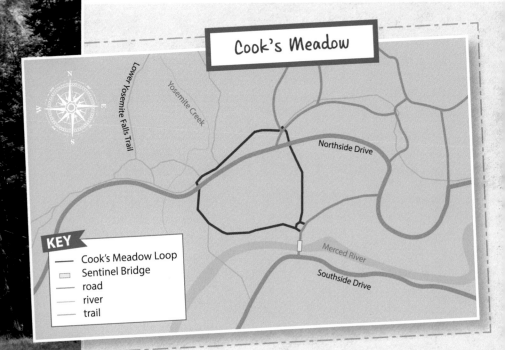

Cook's Meadow

Lower Yosemite Falls Trail

Yosemite Creek

Northside Drive

Merced River

Southside Drive

KEY
— Cook's Meadow Loop
▭ Sentinel Bridge
— road
— river
— trail

glacier—a huge moving body of ice found in mountain valleys or polar regions

valley—an area of low ground between two hills, usually containing a river

landmark—an object in a landscape that can be seen from far away

Visitors walking the loop will pass over the Sentinel Bridge. The bridge is known for its great view of Half Dome. This **granite** dome rises 4,737 feet (1,444 meters) above the valley. The hike to Half Dome is difficult. It is more than 18 miles (29 km) round trip from the Sentinel Bridge.

granite—a very hard rock made up of feldspar, mica, and quartz

FACT: In 1875 climber George Anderson became the first person to reach Half Dome's **summit**. Visitors need special permission to climb Half Dome today.

summit—the highest point of a mountain

The Lower Yosemite Falls Trail is popular in the park. The 1-mile (1.6-km) loop passes by Yosemite Falls. The water travels 2,425 feet (739 m) down. It is North America's tallest waterfall.

Lower Yosemite Falls Trail

Yosemite Falls Trail

Yosemite Falls

Yosemite Creek

Northside Drive

KEY
— Lower Yosemite Falls Trail
☆ Lower Falls Trailhead
— road
— river
— trail
• visitor center

< to El Capitan

Visitors can often spot bear tracks around water sources. Yosemite is famous for its black bears. There are 300 to 500 black bears in the park. They have a great sense of smell, so don't leave food out. Keep a safe distance if you spot a bear.

FACT: Spring is the best time to view Yosemite Falls. Spring rainwater and melted snow flow into the falls.

FACT: There are more than 70 climbing routes on El Capitan. Some routes take days to complete.

At the start of the Lower Yosemite Falls Trail, visitors can find the Valley Loop Trail. The full loop is 13 miles (20.9 km) long. Visitors can also take the half-loop trail, which is 6.5 miles (10.5 km). This trail has a great view of El Capitan. This granite rock rises 3,593 feet (1,095 m) above the valley floor.

Valley Loop Trail

El Capitan

Southside Drive

Northside Drive

Merced River

KEY

—— Valley Loop Trail
—— road
—— river
● visitor center
▲ mountain

Mariposa Grove

The Mariposa Grove is home to hundreds of giant sequoia trees. Visitors hike the Grizzly Giant Loop to see the park's famous sequoias. Sequoias are one of the largest trees on Earth. They can grow to more than 300 feet (91 m) tall.

FACT: Fire plays an important role in the health of the giant sequoias. Their seed pods need fire to open and grow new trees.

GRIZZLY GIANT

About 150 feet (46 m) down the trail is the California Tunnel Tree. A hole was cut into its trunk in 1895. People can walk through the tunnel in the tree.

< The Grizzly Giant is one of Yosemite's oldest trees. It is about 1,800 years old!

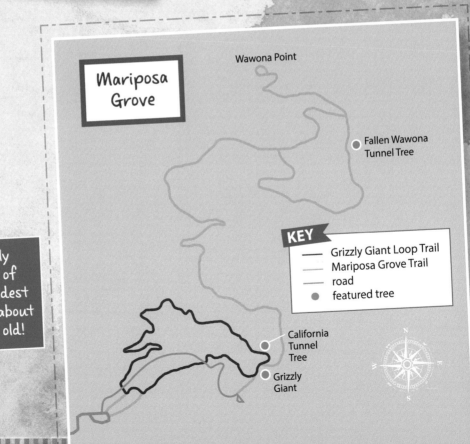

Mariposa Grove

Wawona Point

Fallen Wawona Tunnel Tree

KEY
—— Grizzly Giant Loop Trail
—— Mariposa Grove Trail
—— road
● featured tree

California Tunnel Tree

Grizzly Giant

Tuolumne Meadows

Tuolumne Meadows is Yosemite's largest meadow. The Tuolumne River flows through its green grasses and colorful wildflowers. Visitors can hike the John Muir Trailhead to the Twin Bridges.

FACT: John Muir helped start the Sierra Club in 1892. This club works to protect the park's valley and Mariposa Grove.

Visitors can cross the bridges to the Lyell Canyon to see Mount Lyell. The Lyell Glacier sits atop the mountain. The Lyell Glacier is one of two glaciers left in Yosemite National Park.

FACT: Mount Lyell is the park's highest peak. It rises 13,114 feet (3,997 m).

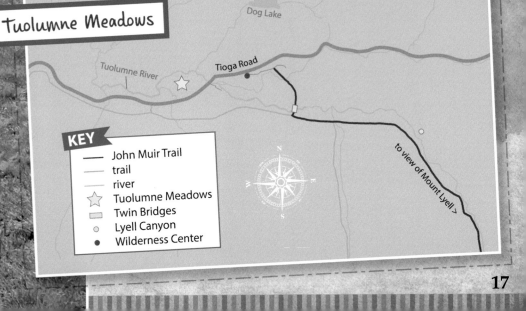

Tuolumne Meadows

Dog Lake

Tuolumne River

Tioga Road

to view of Mount Lyell ›

KEY
— John Muir Trail
— trail
— river
☆ Tuolumne Meadows
▭ Twin Bridges
○ Lyell Canyon
● Wilderness Center

Hetch Hetchy Valley

The Hetch Hetchy Valley is in the northwest corner of the park. Visitors can hike Lookout Point trail through the valley. This 2-mile (3.2-km) trail leads to a rocky landing. The Hetch Hetchy dam can be seen in the distance.

< Hetch Hetchy dam

Visitors pass the Tueeulala and Wapama Falls along the Lookout Point Trail. The falls flow into a **reservoir**.

reservoir—a natural or artificial holding area for storing large amounts of water

Wapama Falls >

^ Tueeulala Falls

FACT: The Hetch Hetchy dam and reservoir were completed in 1923. The reservoir supplies drinking water to the city of San Francisco.

^ mule deer

Many different animals live in Yosemite National Park. Visitors might see mule deer, coyotes, and mountain chickadees.

FACT: The park is also home to the Northern Pacific rattlesnake. Rattlesnakes are **venomous**, so stay away from them.

venomous—able to produce a poison called venom

^ mountain chickadee

About 4 million people visit Yosemite National Park each year. All visitors must help keep Yosemite National Park clean. It's important for future guests and the animals and plants that live there.

Glossary

glacier (GLAY-shur)—a huge moving body of ice found in mountain valleys or polar regions

granite (GRAN-it)—a very hard rock, made up of feldspar, mica, and quartz

landmark (LAND-mark)—an object in a landscape that can be seen from far away

reservoir (REZ-uh-vwar)—a natural or artificial holding area for storing large amounts of water

summit (SUHM-it)—the highest point of a mountain

valley (VAL-ee)—an area of low ground between two hills, usually containing a river

venomous (VEN-uhm-us)—able to produce a poison called venom

Read More

Nagle, Frances. *Yosemite National Park.* Road Trip: National Parks. New York: Gareth Stevens Publishing, 2016.

Rice, Dona. *Travel Adventures: Yosemite.* Huntington Beach, Calif.: Teacher Created Materials, 2018.

Wallace, Audra. *Yosemite National Park.* National Parks. New York: Children's Press, 2018.

Internet Sites

Use FactHound to find Internet sites related to this book:

Visit *www.facthound.com*

Just type in 9781977103574 and go.

Super-cool stuff!

Check out projects, games and lots more at
www.capstonekids.com

Critical Thinking Questions

1. Describe some of the main features of Yosemite National Park.

2. What part of Yosemite National Park would you most like to visit? Why?

3. Why do you think it is important to set aside land for national parks?

Index